Cool Cursive
Handwriting Workbook for TEENS

How to use this Book

This cursive handwriting book is designed for teens or young adults who need to learn, improve or practise their cursive handwriting skills. It is also suitable for beginner adults to master their handwriting skills.

Alphabet Practice

In the first section of this book, you will practice the uppercase and lowercase cursive alphabet. Trace over the dotted letters to learn the letter formation by following the stroke number order in the example given. Afterwards, practice on the thin-lined blank pages to master the letter before moving on to the next letter in the alphabet. The blank lined pages throughout this book have dotted middle lines to help you form the letters correctly and master the letter sizes.

Sentence Practice

In the second section, we provide short sentences for you to practice linking letters to create words and sentences. Trace over the dotted words and then practice on the thin-lined blank pages. You can expand the sentences by adding your own words.

Practice Blank Paper

At the end of this book, blank lined paper is provided to continue practising your cursive writing by writing your own sentences.

Take a Break

Within this workbook, we have also included some images for you to take a break from writing and to have some relaxing fun coloring in. ENJOY!!

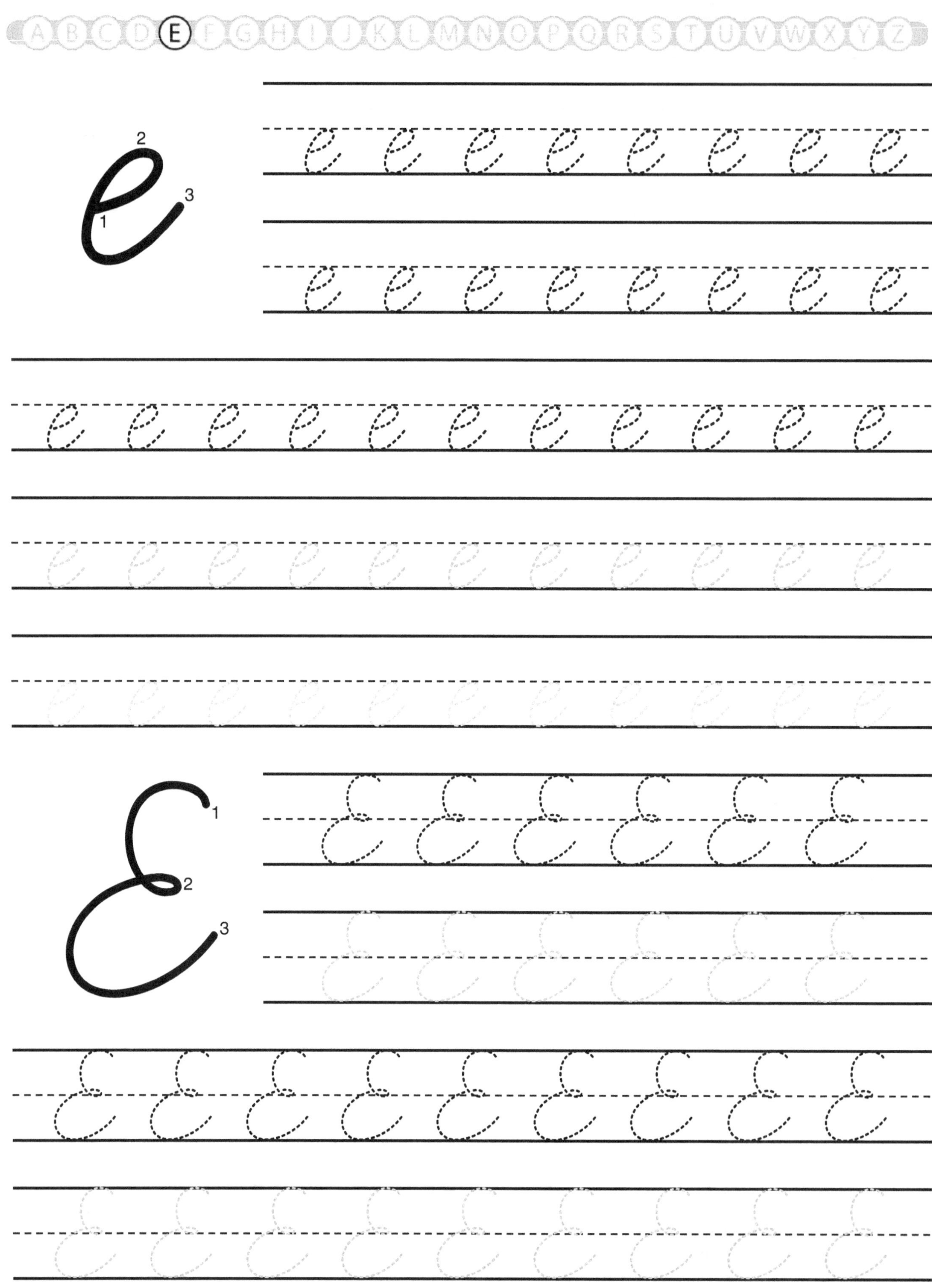

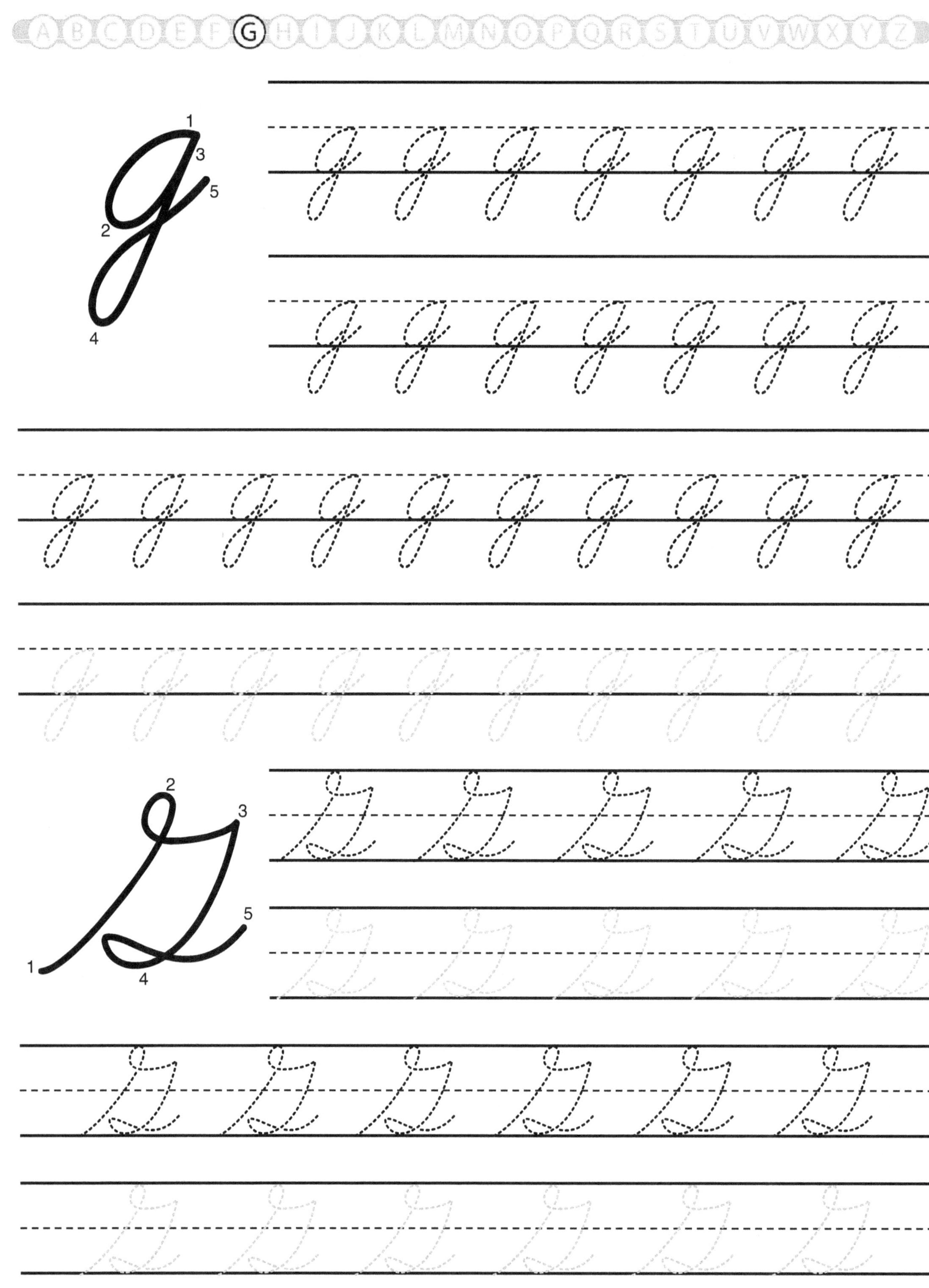

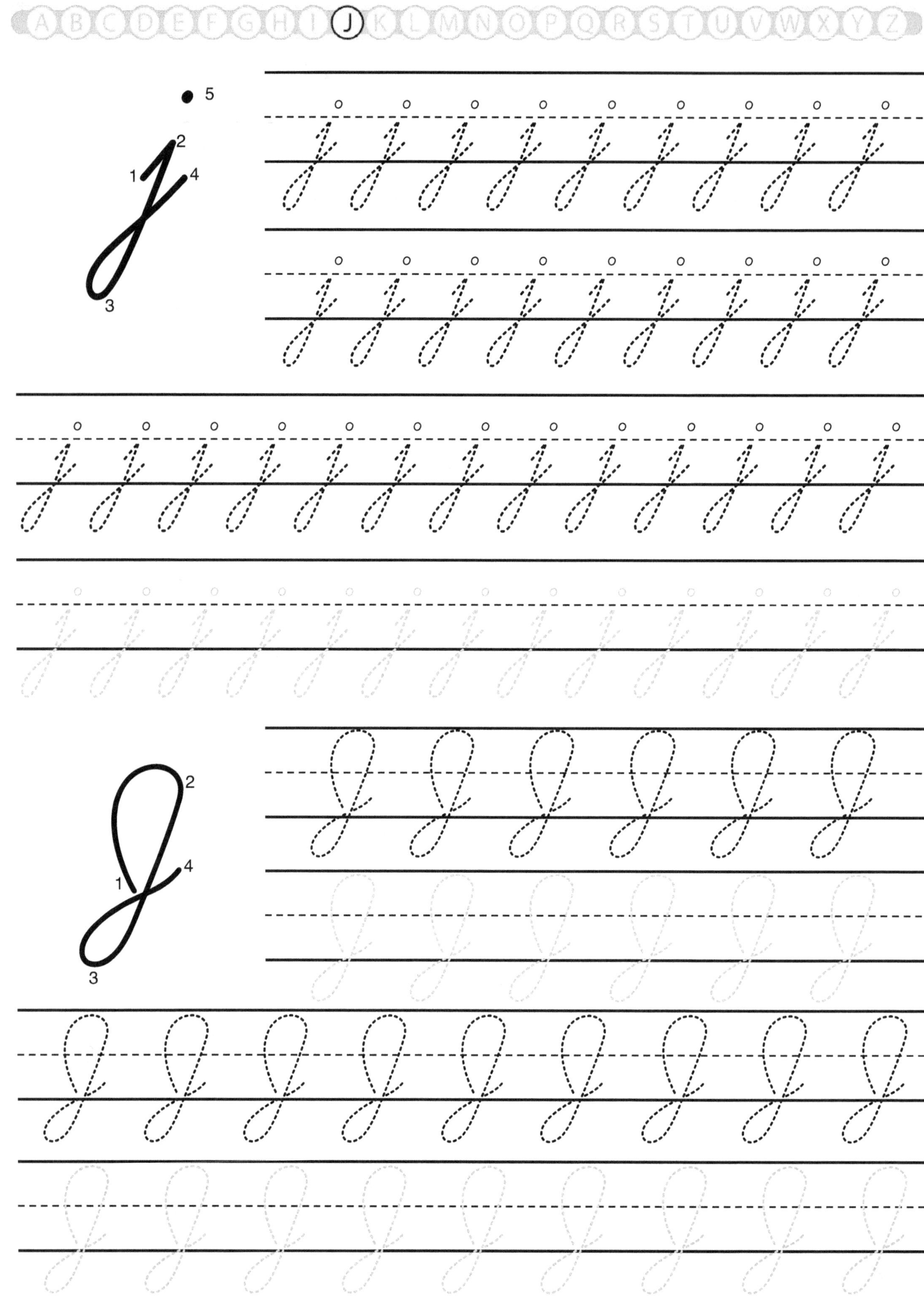

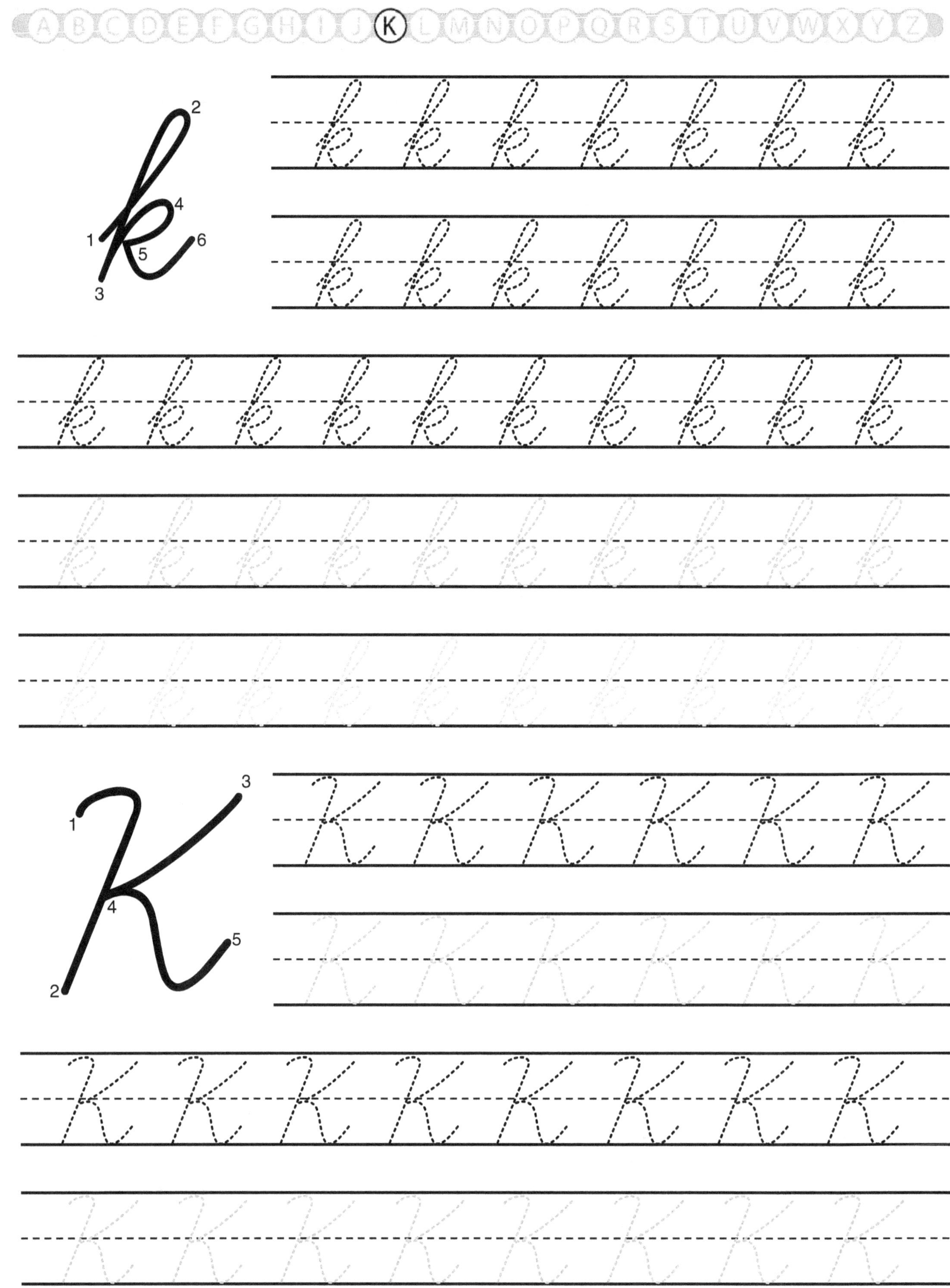

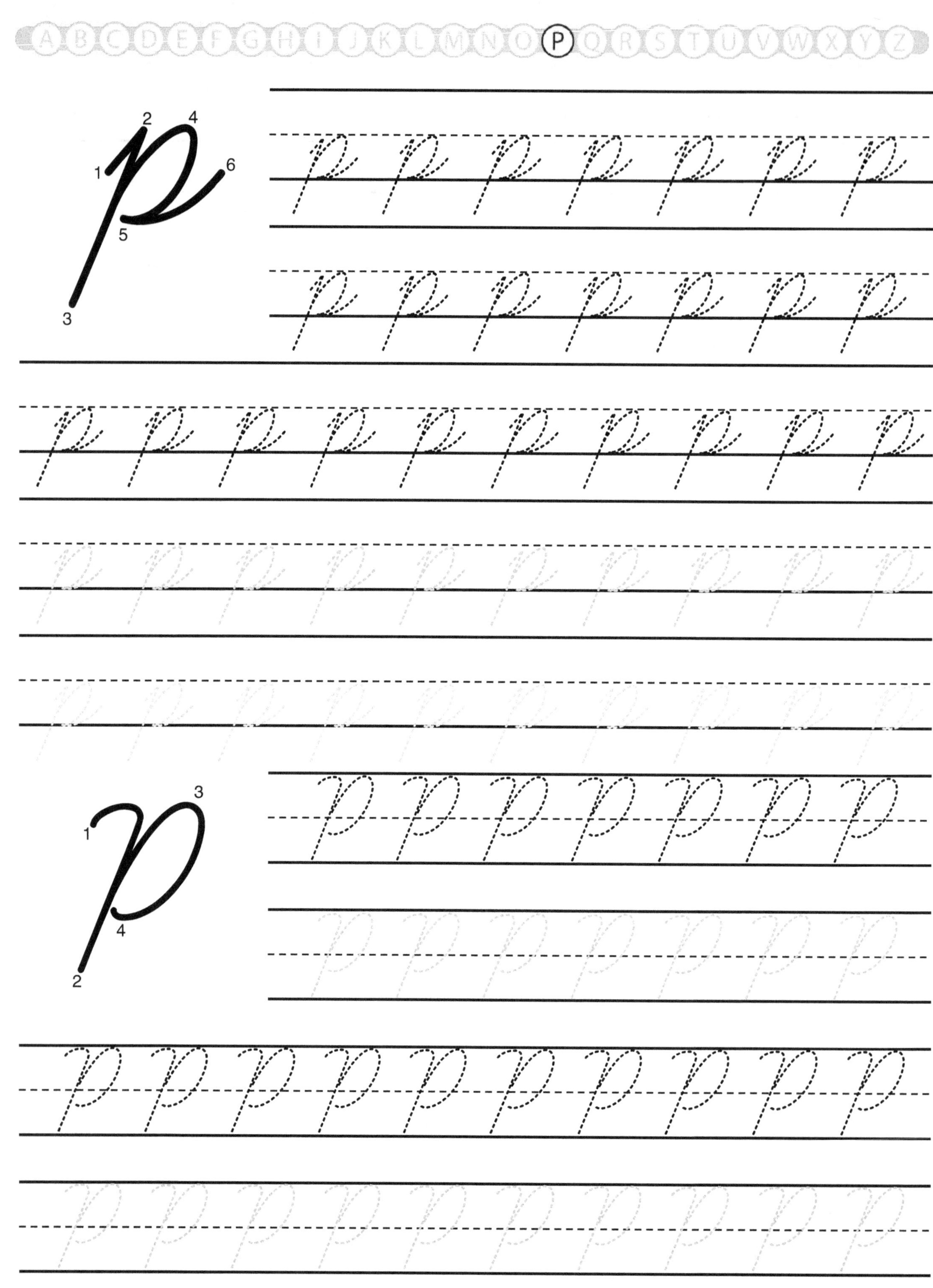

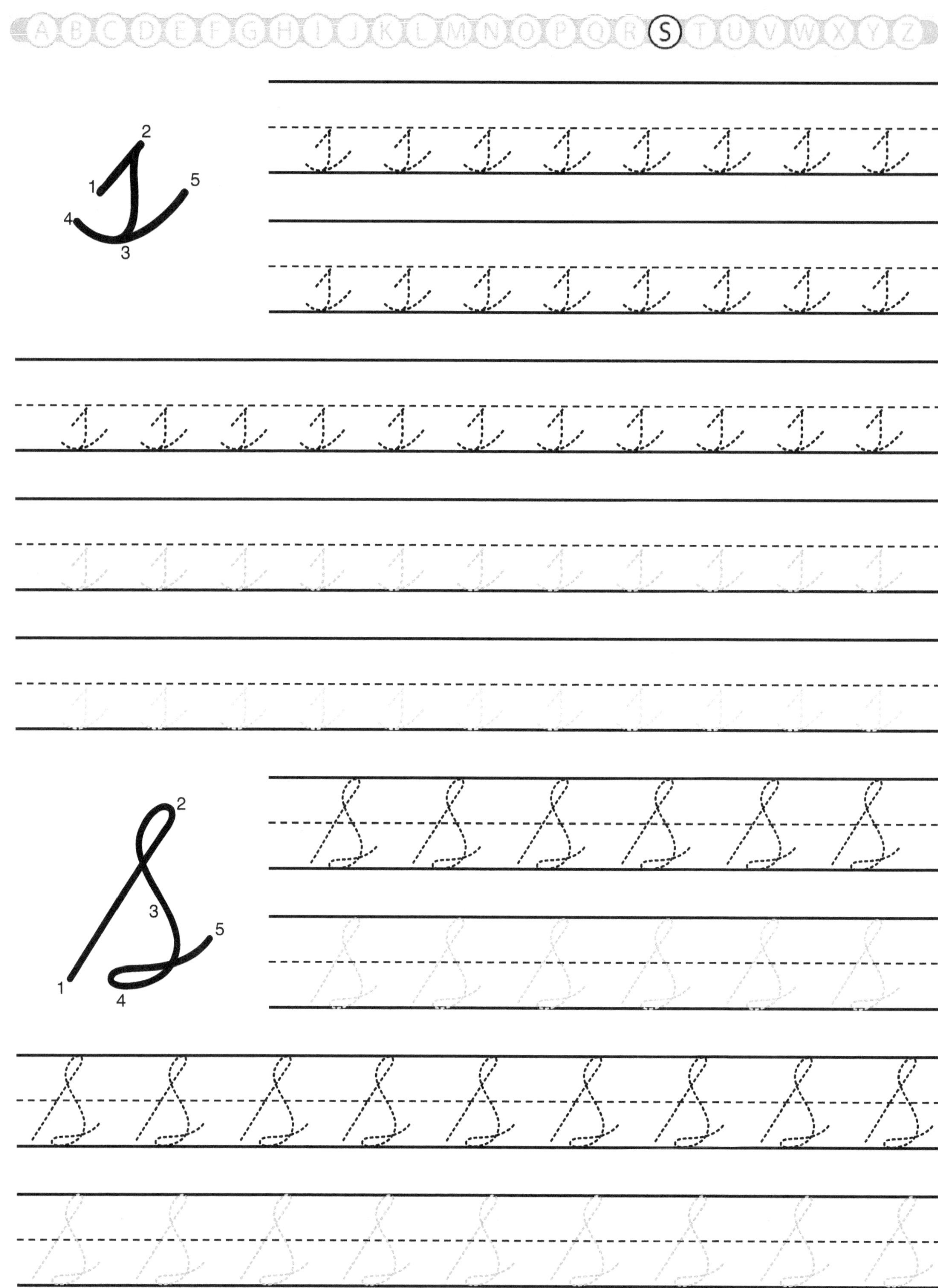

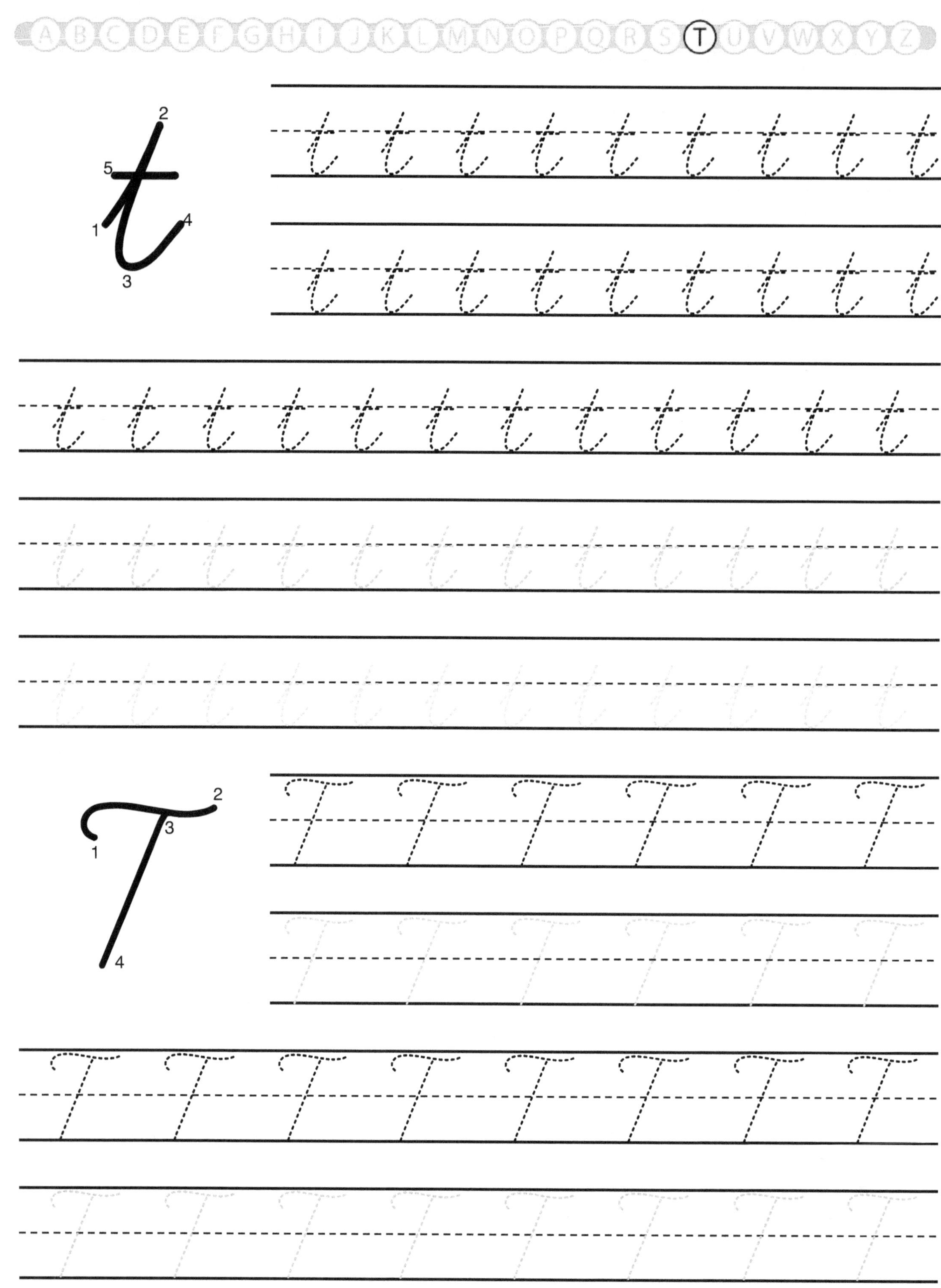

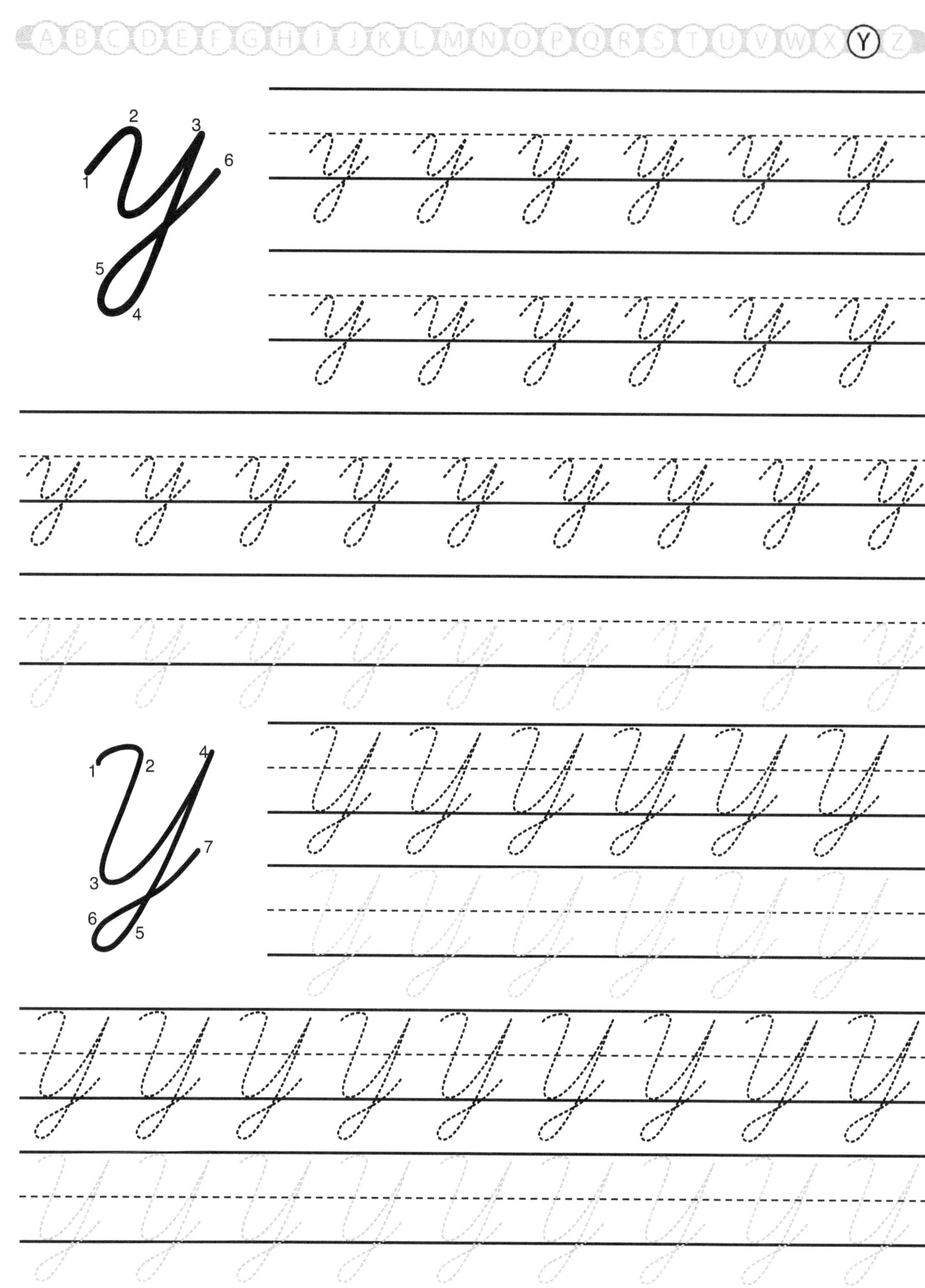

Practice linking letters by tracing over the dotted words, then, re-write the words on the blank lines. The dotted middle line will help you with the letter sizing.

Apples are healthy

TIP: *Cross your t's and dot your i's after you finish writing the word.*

Apricots taste good

Now practice re-writing the sentences on these narrow lines. You can increase the length of the sentence by adding more words of your own.

Practice linking letters by tracing over the dotted words, then, re-write the words on the blank lines. The dotted middle line will help you with the letter sizing.

Behave like a boy

TIP: *You can also link the capital B to the first lowercase letter in the word.*

Back to the basics

Now practice re-writing the sentences on these narrow lines. You can increase the length of the sentence by adding more words of your own.

Practice linking letters by tracing over the dotted words, then, re-write the words on the blank lines. The dotted middle line will help you with the letter sizing.

Catch a crazy crab

TIP: Always link the capital C to the first lowercase letter in the word.

Chalk and cheese

Now practice re-writing the sentences on these narrow lines. You can increase the length of the sentence by adding more words of your own.

Practice linking letters by tracing over the dotted words, then, re-write the words on the blank lines. The dotted middle line will help you with the letter sizing.

Dogs dig up bones

TIP: *You can also link the capital D to the first lowercase letter in the word.*

Drive downtown

Now practice re-writing the sentences on these narrow lines. You can increase the length of the sentence by adding more words of your own.

Practice linking letters by tracing over the dotted words, then, re-write the words on the blank lines. The dotted middle line will help you with the letter sizing.

Enough is enough

TIP: You can cross the letter X, to complete it, after you have finished writing the entire word.

Exceedingly well

Now practice re-writing the sentences on these narrow lines. You can increase the length of the sentence by adding more words of your own.

Practice linking letters by tracing over the dotted words, then, re-write the words on the blank lines. The dotted middle line will help you with the letter sizing.

Feeding frenzy

TIP: *You can also link the capital F, to the first lowercase letter in the word.*

Football is fantastic

Now practice re-writing the sentences on these narrow lines. You can increase the length of the sentence by adding more words of your own.

Practice linking letters by tracing over the dotted words, then, re-write the words on
the blank lines. The dotted middle line will help you with the letter sizing.

Giggling fun girls

TIP: *Name of countries should be written with a capital letter.*

Go to Germany

Now practice re-writing the sentences on these narrow lines. You can increase the length of the sentence by adding more words of your own.

Practice linking letters by tracing over the dotted words, then, re-write the words on the blank lines. The dotted middle line will help you with the letter sizing.

Hello my friend

TIP: Don't lift your pen off the paper when writing the capital H.

House on a hillside

Now practice re-writing the sentences on these narrow lines. You can increase the length of the sentence by adding more words of your own.

Practice linking letters by tracing over the dotted words, then, re-write the words on the blank lines. The dotted middle line will help you with the letter sizing.

Igloos are ice-cold

TIP: You can also link the capital L, to the first lowercase letter in the word.

I imagine it to be

Now practice re-writing the sentences on these narrow lines. You can increase
the length of the sentence by adding more words of your own.

Practice linking letters by tracing over the dotted words, then, re-write the words on the blank lines. The dotted middle line will help you with the letter sizing.

Just jumping jacks

TIP: *Dot your lowercase j after you have finished writing the word.*

Journey to joy

Now practice re-writing the sentences on these narrow lines. You can increase
the length of the sentence by adding more words of your own.

Practice linking letters by tracing over the dotted words, then, re-write the words on the blank lines. The dotted middle line will help you with the letter sizing.

Kings rarely kneel

TIP: *When writing the capital K, you can lift your pen off the paper to write the second stroke.*

Kindness is key

Now practice re-writing the sentences on these narrow lines. You can increase the length of the sentence by adding more words of your own.

Practice linking letters by tracing over the dotted words, then, re-write the words on the blank lines. The dotted middle line will help you with the letter sizing.

Lemons and limes

TIP: When writing the lowercase l, you can start the letter from the lower line.

Laugh out loud

Now practice re-writing the sentences on these narrow lines. You can increase
the length of the sentence by adding more words of your own.

Practice linking letters by tracing over the dotted words, then, re-write the words on
the blank lines. The dotted middle line will help you with the letter sizing.

Miracles are made

TIP: *When writing the capital M, it's best to not lift your pen off the paper.*

Movies with music

Now practice re-writing the sentences on these narrow lines. You can increase the length of the sentence by adding more words of your own.

Practice linking letters by tracing over the dotted words, then, re-write the words on the blank lines. The dotted middle line will help you with the letter sizing.

No names given

TIP: *When writing the capital N, it should always be linked to the next letter.*

News at noontime

Now practice re-writing the sentences on these narrow lines. You can increase the length of the sentence by adding more words of your own.

Practice linking letters by tracing over the dotted words, then, re-write the words on the blank lines. The dotted middle line will help you with the letter sizing.

Only once a year

TIP: *When writing the capital O, you can link it to the next lowercase letter.*

Over and out

Now practice re-writing the sentences on these narrow lines. You can increase the length of the sentence by adding more words of your own.

Practice linking letters by tracing over the dotted words, then, re-write the words on the blank lines. The dotted middle line will help you with the letter sizing.

Pandas are pretty

TIP: When writing the capital P, you need to lift your pen off the paper to write the next letter in the word. Though the second letter can be linked to the P.

Picture perfect day

Now practice re-writing the sentences on these narrow lines. You can increase the length of the sentence by adding more words of your own.

Practice linking letters by tracing over the dotted words, then, re-write the words on the blank lines. The dotted middle line will help you with the letter sizing.

Queens questions

TIP: When writing the lowercase q, don't lift your pen off the paper to write the next letter in the word.

Quit quarrelling

Now practice re-writing the sentences on these narrow lines. You can increase
the length of the sentence by adding more words of your own.

Practice linking letters by tracing over the dotted words, then, re-write the words on the blank lines. The dotted middle line will help you with the letter sizing.

Rabbits are not red

TIP: When writing the capital R, you can lift your pen off the paper to write the second stroke.

Rock and roll time

Now practice re-writing the sentences on these narrow lines. You can increase the length of the sentence by adding more words of your own.

Practice linking letters by tracing over the dotted words, then, re-write the words on the blank lines. The dotted middle line will help you with the letter sizing.

Sunshine and sea

Summer is so hot

Now practice re-writing the sentences on these narrow lines. You can increase the length of the sentence by adding more words of your own.

Practice linking letters by tracing over the dotted words, then, re-write the words on the blank lines. The dotted middle line will help you with the letter sizing.

Ten times the price

TIP: *When writing the capital T, you can link it to the next lowercase letter.*

Tiptoe around them

Now practice re-writing the sentences on these narrow lines. You can increase
the length of the sentence by adding more words of your own.

Practice linking letters by tracing over the dotted words, then, re-write the words on the blank lines. The dotted middle line will help you with the letter sizing.

Under the unicorn

TIP: *When writing the capital U, keep your pen on the paper when moving onto the next letter.*

Understand the user

Now practice re-writing the sentences on these narrow lines. You can increase the length of the sentence by adding more words of your own.

Practice linking letters by tracing over the dotted words, then, re-write the words on the blank lines. The dotted middle line will help you with the letter sizing.

Very violent crime

TIP: *When writing the capital V, you may link the letter to the next lowercase letter.*

Vases versus plates

Now practice re-writing the sentences on these narrow lines. You can increase the length of the sentence by adding more words of your own.

Practice linking letters by tracing over the dotted words, then, re-write the words on the blank lines. The dotted middle line will help you with the letter sizing.

Wicked witches

TIP: When writing the capital W, you may link the lower part of the letter to the next lowercase letter.

Washing a white car

Now practice re-writing the sentences on these narrow lines. You can increase the length of the sentence by adding more words of your own.

Practice linking letters by tracing over the dotted words, then, re-write the words on the blank lines. The dotted middle line will help you with the letter sizing.

X-rays are pricey

TIP: *When writing the capital X, remember to write the single diagonal stroke first, top to bottom, before the second stroke that links to the next letter.*

Xylophone music

Now practice re-writing the sentences on these narrow lines. You can increase the length of the sentence by adding more words of your own.

Practice linking letters by tracing over the dotted words, then, re-write the words on the blank lines. The dotted middle line will help you with the letter sizing.

Your car is yellow

TIP: *When writing the capital Y, remember to keep your pen on the paper and flow to the next letter.*

Yams are yummy

Now practice re-writing the sentences on these narrow lines. You can increase the length of the sentence by adding more words of your own.

Practice linking letters by tracing over the dotted words, then, re-write the words on the blank lines. The dotted middle line will help you with the letter sizing.

Zoos have zebras

Zip past the zombie

Now practice re-writing the sentences on these narrow lines. You can increase the length of the sentence by adding more words of your own.

Take a BREAK
Color me in

Take a BREAK
Color me in

Take a BREAK
Color me in

Take a BREAK
Color me in

Take a BREAK
Color me in

Take a BREAK

Color me in